THE BIG RED BARN SPEAKS . . .

The Story of the Flight 93 Barn

Written by Sally Musser Zeigler

AuthorHouse™
1663 Liberty Drive
Bloomington, IN 47403
www.authorhouse.com
Phone: 833-262-8899

Because of the dynamic nature of the Internet, any web addresses or links contained in this book may have changed since publication and may no longer be valid. The views expressed in this work are solely those of the author and do not necessarily reflect the views of the publisher, and the publisher hereby disclaims any responsibility for them.

This book is printed on acid-free paper.

ISBN: 978-1-4918-7702-9 (sc)
ISBN: 978-1-4918-8618-2 (e)

Print information available on the last page.

Published by AuthorHouse   11/26/2022

authorHOUSE®

Dedicated to my parents, Robert and Phyllis Musser
To whom the Big Red Barn meant so much

Also dedicated to my husband, Don Zeigler
Who gave me his total support for this project

Thanks to Josh Spangler and Derek Hoyman
Who gave me their encouragement

Lastly, dedicated to the Heroes of United Flight 93
Who gave their lives to save others on 9/11/2001

Many years ago, around the year 1850, men worked long and hard placing beams and hammering boards so that I, The Big Red Barn, could take shape. I am tall and painted bright red so that people can see me from far away. At this moment, the memories begin to form in my mind's eye. I have seen and heard so many things within my walls. My memories are of years gone by. Of people come and gone. IF ONLY I COULD SPEAK . . . . .

It was that time of year again. Summer was almost over, and fall was just around the corner. The farmer was returning from the field with a fresh load of hay to be stored in the hay mow for the winter. Oh, how useful I am! Upstairs, I store hay, straw, and oats for the animals. Downstairs, I am home for many animals such as cows, chickens, horses, pigs, and, of course, mommy cats and their kittens.

"I love the sights and smells inside my walls." thought the Big, Red Barn. There's usually a cool calmness here, but not today. There is an ominous roar of thunder nearby. I can see the dark sky through my windows. I see the twister coming as my farmer, Mr. Stutzman returns home from selling his fruits and vegetables at market. He is a "huckster" by trade. I want to shout "LOOK OUT!" But the tornado strikes too quickly. I try to hold my walls together as much as I can, but a beam twists and falls on my farmer while he is still holding his little boy's hand. I think, "OH NO! Please let him survive!" But he's gone. The little boy screams, but at least he is safe.

The next day, a steady stream of horses and buggies from far and wide park along the road. People even walk to see the destruction. Hams from the smokehouse are strewn across the fields; windows are blown out of the farmhouse. I feel so sad and miserable that I didn't withstand that tragic tornado. I hope with all my heart that perhaps someone will rebuild me in the days to come.

My wish of being rebuilt has come true. My beams and walls have been replaced. The only sad reminder that remains from the tornado is some twisted beams the men reused. But there are happier times now. You see, a new family has come to live here. There are two brothers and two sisters. The oldest brother's name is Arthur and his sisters' names are Thelma and Marlene. The other brother named Karl loves to play basketball! His dad owns a lumber mill, so they nailed down a hardwood floor and hung a hoop upstairs. It's exciting when Karl's friends come to practice after school and on Saturdays. I think it's quite unique that I have a basketball court within my walls. I'd like to shout, "Good shot, Karl! Way to rebound!"

Many more years have gone by since Karl played basketball upstairs, and many more children have played here within my walls. I love the animals, but the children hold a special place in my heart. The year is 1956, and yet another new family lives here now. Bob and Phyllis and their children have made this their home. It is such a coincidence that Phyllis's mother, who was a little girl when the tornado destroyed me, came to see me with her family in their horse and buggy many years ago. Another coincidence is that Bob works at the lumber company for Karl and Arthur who used to play inside my walls! Arthur is even Bob's uncle since he married Bob's aunt. This new family and I have a lot of connections already!

Randy, Roger, Sally, and Ronnie love to look for kittens in the hay mow. They spend hours swinging on a rope that their dad, Bob, has tied to the beam. They climb the ladder to the top of the hay mow. "BE CAREFUL!" I try to shout. Then they grab the rope and jump from the ladder! Way out over the hay they sway. At the highest point, they let go and fall into the hay! What wonderful fun it is!

Many things are changing in my neighborhood. A lake has been built right beside me. It's called Indian Lake. I've become a landmark of sorts. When people give directions they always say, "Turn left at the big, red barn." Families from the city have bought lots at the lake, and built summer homes. The lake children are drawn to me like magnets! They come to feed the cows, pet the kittens, and brush the horses and ponies. Bob's children and I have made many new friends. You know how I love children! Randy, Roger, Sally, and Ronnie decide to have a carnival. The lake kids come and pay quarters to ride Princie, my pony. Princie can jump over hay bales. The kids squeal in delight. They shoot hoops and swing on my rope upstairs. Oh, what happy days!

One of my favorite things is when Bob, the farmer, keeps horses for other people. I can help him earn some extra money for his family. My favorite horse is Randy's horse named Applejack. He and Princie are friends with two other horses named Peso and Taffy. Bob and I love the smell of horses and ponies inside my walls. They smell much better than the pigs and chickens Bob sometimes brings home! Cows are also interesting animals. The other day, a bull that was being loaded onto a truck got so scared that he jumped right through my window. What a strange sight!

After a while, Bob thinks of another way to earn extra money for the family. The lake people need a place to store their boats during the winter. So Bob puts as many as eleven boats upstairs. My floors creak from all the extra weight. You'll never guess what else Bob stores upstairs; an old-fashioned fire truck! Randy, Roger, Sally and Ronnie like to turn the crank for the siren to blare. Oh, you should hear how it echoes through my walls!

Bob likes to do woodworking too. He has saws, hammers, and other tools upstairs. In his spare time, he makes birdhouses, crates, stools, hat racks, and many other items. The smell of freshly cut wood is always a special treat. Bob and his wife, Phyllis, have lived here for 55 years. Their children are grown up and now the grandchildren and great grandchildren come to visit. Bob loves to give the grandkids tractor rides on his favorite tractor. I guess Bob and I both love children!

Just the other day, Bob bought a new pony for the grandchildren to ride. This little pony looks just like my old friend Princie. Bob and Phyllis named him Prince, and Bob made a new wooden sign to hang on the door of his pen. When Bob brought Prince home, the grandchildren rode on the back of the truck holding the baby pony to keep it safe. I'm so glad to have a new friend to live here with me.

You'll never guess what happened next. One early fall day, September 11, 2001 to be exact, something occurred that has made me more than just a landmark. I simply can't believe it, but I became famous around the world. It was a sad and unusual day. It started out perfectly. The sky was a beautiful blue with soft white clouds and bright sunshine. I heard a loud boom, and I began to shake. I thought, "OH NO, not another tornado to knock me down!" But then I stopped shaking and saw a big cloud shaped like a mushroom in the sky. What could that be? Was there an explosion?

My neighbor took a picture of me with the mushroom cloud in the sky above me. She had heard the boom and felt the ground rumble, too. It turns out that a huge airplane crashed while terrorists were on board. Terrorists are people who want to do harm to others. A group of brave passengers tried to take the plane back, but it crashed before they could save it. Those passengers became heroes for standing up against the terrorists. The whole world changed on this day. My picture now hangs in The Smithsonian Institute in Washington, D.C. as well as many other special places around the world as a reminder of what happened on September 11, 2001. A war on terrorism has begun. Our world will never be the same.

More than ten years have passed since United Airlines Flight 93 crashed in a field near Shanksville, Pennsylvania so close to me. Every year thousands of visitors from all over the world come to see the new Flight 93 Memorial which has become a National Park. My farmer, Bob, isn't with me anymore. His wife Phyllis, his family, and I miss him very much. Things are very quiet now. I still have a few mommy cats, several kittens, and two miniature horses that live with me. Bob and Phyllis's grown children, grandchildren and great grandchildren stop by to visit. Even some of the lake kids still come to pet the kittens. I wonder every day who will be the next family to make memories with me. What will the future hold for me? I just hope it's a family with children. You know how I love children!

Printed in the United States
by Baker & Taylor Publisher Services